DATE DUE			

JOHN PAUL II
The Pilgrim Pope

Author
Robert W. Douglas

 Childrens Press, Chicago

Printed with Ecclesiastical Approbation

Copyright © 1980 by Regensteiner Publishing Enterprises, Inc.
All rights reserved. Published simultaneously in Canada.
Printed in the United States of America.

2 3 4 5 6 7 8 9 10 11 12 R 86 85 84 83

Library of Congress Cataloging in Publication Data

Douglas, Robert W.
  John Paul II, the Pilgrim Pope.

  SUMMARY: Describes the life of Karol Cardinal
Wojtyla of Poland, including his election as Pope John
Paul II, his travels as a pastoral pope, and his effect
on people around the world.
  1. John Paul II, Pope, 1920-   —Juvenile literature.
2. Popes—Biography—Juvenile literature. [1. John
Paul II, Pope, 1920-   2. Popes] I. Title.
BX1378.5.D68   262'.13'0924 [B] [92]   79-24930
ISBN 0-516-03563-0

Dedicated to the memory of

Ted Winter

JOHN PAUL II

They call him the pilgrim pope. He is John Paul II. In October, 1978, he was chosen to lead the Roman Catholic Church. One year later he had already traveled three times to faraway countries. He brought joy and hope to millions of people. Most of them would never be able to see him in Rome. He came to them. John Paul II has been reaching out to people all of his life.

The official investiture of Pope John Paul II took place on October 22, 1978, in Rome. He was the first non-Italian to be elected pope in more than 450 years.

R. Darolle/Sygma

The future pope, on his mother's knee, was only a few months old when this photograph was taken.

He was born May 18, 1920, in a small town in the south of Poland. He was named Carolus Joseph Wojtyla (voy•TEE•wah) and called Karol or Lolek. His mother died when he was nine years old. Karol's older brother was a doctor. He died of scarlet fever. Karol and his father were alone. Karol's father took care of him. He made sure Karol went to Mass every day, was always on time for school, and did his homework. There wasn't much time to play. But when there was, Karol played soccer. He liked hiking, skiing, and canoeing too. But most of all he liked soccer.

Marc Pokempner/Black Star

Cardinal Cody smiled as John Paul II received a warm welcome from the people of Chicago.

James Andanson/Sygma

Young Karol (circled) posed in 1930 with the other members of his school class in Poland. The man to Karol's right is his father, Mr. Wojtyla.

Karol did well in school. He was good at languages. He especially liked reading stories and poems about Poland. Sometimes the smartest ones in class are not well liked. It was different with Karol. He made many friends. He wasn't a show-off.

In Karol's school everyone studied religion. These lessons were taught by priests. They noticed Karol. They thought he would make a good priest. But Karol had other ideas.

Sipa-Press/Black Star

John Paul II blessed Polish schoolchildren during his pilgrimage to the sacred Mount Jasna Gora, a shrine which symbolizes the birth of Christianity in Poland.

Karol had special talent. He could act very well. Whenever a play was given at his school, he had an important part. Folk dancing and singing were part of Karol's life too. He even wrote poetry. Later some books of his poems were printed.

When Karol was eighteen, he moved with his father to the city of Krakow. He began to study drama. He was part of a famous theater workshop. His friends felt sure he would become an actor.

Black Star

During his visit to the Cathedral of the Immaculate Conception of the Blessed Virgin Mary in Philadelphia, John Paul II celebrated Mass with members of the community.

Karol's college life came to a sudden end in 1939. World War II began. Poland was overrun by German soldiers. Poles were no longer free. They were forced to work for the Germans. Karol became a stonecutter.

Young Poles began meeting secretly. They wanted to keep their religion alive. If they were discovered, they would be arrested or killed. Yet many young men met and formed prayer groups. Karol belonged to a prayer group. At about that time, Karol changed his mind about becoming an actor. He decided he would be a priest. But all schools in Poland were closed. The Germans would not allow anyone to study for the priesthood. Karol began his studies in secret.

Diego Goldberg/Sygma
Two children reached out to greet John Paul II as he walked down a street in Mexico.

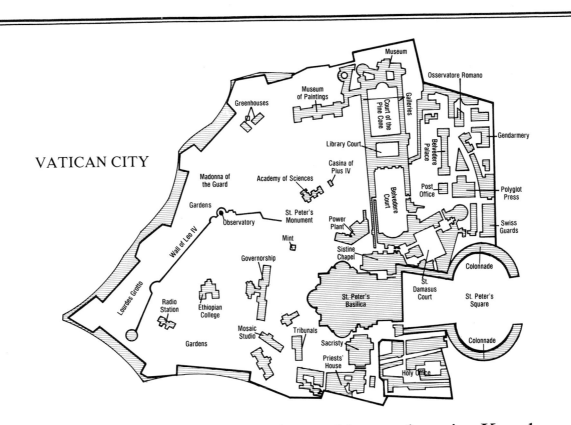

VATICAN CITY

After the war ended, people could travel again. Karol was sent to Rome, Italy. Rome is an important place to Catholics. The tiny state called the Vatican is there. It is like a kingdom and the pope is its ruler. Important Catholic leaders meet there. They help the pope decide church matters. Catholics from all over the world travel to the Vatican. They want to see the pope and receive his blessing.

Karol continued his studies in Rome. He learned to speak Italian. Later he spent time in France. There he learned to speak French. He studied many languages so he could talk with people wherever he went. He learned all he could about helping people. He wanted to be a good priest.

John Paul II paused for a thoughtful moment before beginning Mass in Metropolitan Cathedral in Mexico City. Behind him is the papal chair which he brought with him from Rome.

In 1948 Father Karol Wojtyla returned to Poland. Many people in his parish needed food and clothing. Many were sick. There were not enough hospitals. The young priest did everything he could to help them. He never seemed to want comforts for himself. He rode a bicycle and lived very simply. He did not change even when he became a bishop. He still went hiking and skiing. People expected him to dress in proper robes and live in a fine home, but he didn't. When he was made archbishop of Krakow, he had to live in the palace. But he turned it into a place where everyone could come. He found new ways to care for people's needs.

Wherever he traveled, crowds of people gathered to see the man known as the Pilgrim Pope.

The papal crest or coat of arms appears on many objects used by the pope.

When he was elected pope, he had already been a cardinal for eleven years. He had been at the Vatican many times. The other cardinals all knew him. They believed he was the best man to lead the church. But Pope John Paul II surprised them. He began his rule by talking to the people, not just giving his blessing. Things would never be the same.

As pope, John Paul II is the religious leader of Catholics in countries all over the world. He wants to do more than lead people. He wants to go to them, speak with them, and know them. He loves them.

C. Simonpietri/Sygma

John Paul II waved to the crowd that gathered to greet him when he visited his homeland of Poland. His special open-air car has been nicknamed the "popemobile."

Father Karol Wojtyla became a priest in 1946.

John Paul's first pilgrimage was to Mexico and the Dominican Republic in January, 1979. People there were able to understand his message. He spoke in their language.

Six months later he traveled to Poland. He was no longer a Polish archbishop. Now he was head of the Vatican and the Roman Catholic Church. He went to his home city, Krakow. He met with government leaders. He visited shrines. Best of all, he was able to visit his old friends.

Thousands of people lined the streets and a few lucky ones looked through nearby windows to see John Paul II when he visited Mexico.

A young mentally handicapped girl in Ireland received the blessing of Pope John Paul II as he laid his hand on her forehead.

John Paul flew to Ireland in September. Many people gathered to hear him speak. The pope has a great love for children. Wherever he goes, he shows it. In Ireland he visited some special children. Some were blind, some deaf, some crippled. He blessed them.

In October the pope traveled to the United States. Churches in places he would visit were cleaned and decorated. Altars were built where he would celebrate Mass. Choirs and bands practiced special music. People put up banners and signs of welcome.

John Paul II kissed the ground, a sign of respect and humility, after landing in Boston, Massachusetts. He has done this in every country he has visited.

People lined the streets to see John Paul II. Many who were not Catholics came. They had heard about the pilgrim pope. They wanted to see this leader who cared so much about people.

The crowds chanted, "We want the pope!" When he came in sight they called out, "Long live the pope!" Some people sang a Polish song, "Sto Lat." It means "May you live 100 years." It made John Paul happy to hear those words. Young people cheered the pope as they would a hero: "John Paul II, we love you!"

Gerald Cross
John Paul II often used a U. S. Marine Corps helicopter to travel from one place to another during his United States visit.

Children, especially babies, have always had a
special place in the heart of John Paul II.

Thousands and thousands came to where the pope would
celebrate Mass. They came early and carried blankets, picnic
chairs, and lunches. No one seemed to mind waiting. It
would be worth it to see the pope. While they waited, people
sang songs. Children dressed in clothes of other lands
performed folk dances. Some people prayed.

People brought the pope gifts. Some were handmade, like
a warm sweater for him to wear skiing. There were gifts of
flowers and food, like bread made from wheat just harvested.
Young people brought things like blue jeans, a soccer ball,
and even a guitar.

Young children in New York City gathered around
John Paul II to receive his blessing.

Papal Vestments

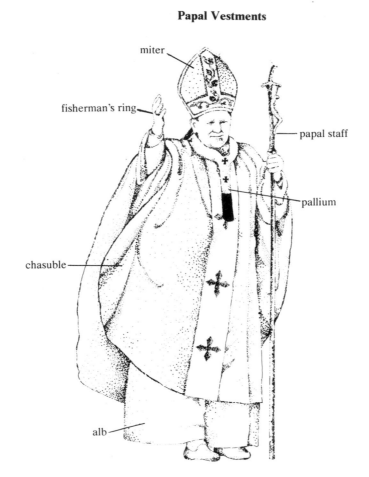

miter

fisherman's ring

papal staff

pallium

chasuble

alb

Pope John Paul II blessed the people. He spoke about working for peace and talked about helping those in need. He said Christians everywhere should work and pray together. He spoke to Catholics about their religion. But what he was saying was important to all the people. His voice was heard across the land.

John Paul II became the second pope in history to address the United Nations when he visited New York City in October, 1979.

Each time a crowd gathered, John Paul stayed to greet them. He never seemed tired. He stood smiling, waving, blessing the people. During one farewell, he looked down from where he was standing. He copied the rhythm of the chant he had heard so often. "John Paul II, he loves you!" he called out. "John Paul II, he loves you!"

John Paul's whole life has been like a pilgrimage. He moved from one milestone to another. Finally he reached the highest position of his church. But John Paul II didn't see this as the end. It was a new beginning. As John Paul II has shown the world, he is a man who keeps moving.

Gerald Cross
A tired John Paul II waved good-night to the crowd from the balcony of the cardinal's residence in Chicago.

Important Events in the Life of John Paul II

1920	Born May 18 in Wadowice, Poland
1938	Moved to Krakow; began to study drama
1939	Study interrupted by World War II
1940	Began work in stone quarry; joined underground groups of the Resistance Movement
1942	Began studying for the priesthood
1946	Ordained a priest November 1; sent to Rome for further study
1948	Returned to Poland; served as priest and teacher
1958	Became bishop
1964	Became archbishop of Krakow
1967	Made a cardinal by Pope Paul VI
1978	Elected pope October 16
1979	Began a series of pilgrimages outside Italy
1981	Was shot during an audience in Vatican Square; recovered and returned to his duties

GLOSSARY

These words are defined the way they are used in this book.

altar	a table or raised place used in a religious service
archbishop	the highest ranking bishop
bishop	the head of a church district
cardinal	the most important Roman Catholic official after the pope
drama	a course of study that deals with plays and acting
Krakow	a city in Poland known especially for its schools
Mass	the main religious ceremony in the Roman Catholic Church
milestone	an important happening in a person's life
parish	an area that has its own church
pilgrim	a person who travels to a special place for a religious purpose
pilgrimage	the journey of a pilgrim
pope	the person who is head of the Roman Catholic Church
priest	a clergyman of the Roman Catholic Church
religion	belief in God or worship of God
Rome	the capital city of Italy
shrine	a holy place for worshiping God
talent	a natural ability to do something
theater workshop	a place where actors learn to perform
Vatican	the part of Rome, Italy, which is a separate state and is the home of the Roman Catholic Church